COURAGE

COURAGE

EDITED BY
BENJAMIN UNSETH

COURAGE, THE LITTLE BOOKS OF VIRTUE, SERIES ONE

Edited by Benjamin Unseth

P. O. Box 20132, Bloomington, MN 55420

ISBN 1-881830-19-5

The courage we desire and prize is not the courage to die decently but to live manfully.

THOMAS CARLYLE

Courage is resistance to fear, mastery of fear—not absence of fear. Except a creature be part coward, it is not a compliment to say it is brave.

MARK TWAIN
Pudd'nhead Wilson

AT TIMES HE REGARDED THE WOUNDED SOLDIERS IN AN ENVIOUS WAY. HE CONCEIVED PERSONS WITH TORN BODIES TO BE PECULIARLY HAPPY. HE WISHED THAT HE, TOO, HAD A WOUND, A RED BADGE OF COURAGE.

STEPHEN CRANE

Without belittling the courage with which men have died, we should not forget those acts of courage with which men...have lived. The courage of life is often a less dramatic spectacle than the courage of a final moment; but it is no less a magnificent mixture of triumph and tragedy. A man does what he must—in spite of personal consequences, in spite of obstacles and dangers and pressures—and that is the basis of all human morality.... In whatever arena of life one may meet the challenge of courage, whatever may be the sacrifices he faces if he follows his conscience—the loss of his friends, his fortune, his contentment, even the esteem of his fellow men—each man must decide for himself the course he will follow. The stories of past courage can define that ingredient—they can teach, they can offer hope, they can provide inspiration. But they cannot supply courage itself. For this each man must look into his own soul. ❁

JOHN F. KENNEDY

That's one small step for a man, one great leap for mankind.

NEIL ARMSTRONG, AMERICAN ASTRONAUT

First words spoken on the moon

Death and sorrow will be the companions of our journey; hardship our garment; constancy and valor our only shield.... We must be undaunted, we must be inflexible.

WINSTON CHURCHILL

Report on the war, House of Commons

PSALM 27 TLB

The Lord is my light and my salvation; he protects me from danger—whom shall I fear? When evil men come to destroy me, they will stumble and fall! Yes, though a mighty army marches against me, my heart shall know no fear! I am confident that God will save me.

The one thing I want from God, the thing I seek most of all, is the privilege of…living in his presence every day of my life, delighting in his incomparable perfections and glory. There I'll be when troubles come. He will hide me. He will set me on a high rock out of reach of all my enemies. Then I will bring him sacrifices and sing his praises with much joy.

Listen to my pleading, Lord! Be merciful and send the help I need….

Tell me what to do, O Lord, and make it plain because I am surrounded by waiting enemies.... I am expecting the Lord to rescue me again, so that once again I will see his goodness to me here in the land of the living.

Don't be impatient. Wait for the Lord, and he will come and save you! Be brave, stouthearted and courageous. ❁

Be steadfast, my boy, when you're tempted,
To do what you know to be right.
Stand firm by the colors of manhood,
And you will o'ercome in the fight.
"The right," be your battle cry ever
In waging the warfare of life,
And God, who knows who are the heroes,
Will give you the strength for the strife. ❁

PHOEBE CARY

Our Heroes

A MAN SHOULD STOP HIS EARS AGAINST PARALYZING TERROR, AND RUN THE RACE THAT IS SET BEFORE HIM WITH A SINGLE MIND.

ROBERT LOUIS STEVENSON

No coward soul is mine,

No trembler in the world's storm-troubled sphere:

I see Heaven's glories shine,

And faith shines equal, arming me from fear.

EMILY BRONTË

Last Lines

One hot, dusty morning, Goliath, a nine-foot giant, marched out from the Philistine camp to mock the Israelite army, as he had done for several days. He carried his enormous spear with an iron point that weighed fifteen pounds. Worn down from fighting off the Philistine's attacks and the giant's threats, King Saul and all his Israelite soldiers were terrified. A shepherd boy named

David, who didn't have any armor and had never fought in a battle, was the only Israelite willing to face Goliath.

With only five small, smooth stones as his ammunition, David took his sling and went out to meet Goliath. "Am I a dog that you come at me with sticks?" demanded Goliath. Echoes of the giant's laughter thundered through the valley, as Goliath watched David running toward him with his sling swinging in the air.

When David finally let the stone fly from his sling, it went whistling through the air until it hit the giant so hard in his forehead that it stuck there. For a breath-taking moment the giant swayed, and then suddenly, Goliath fell facedown onto the dusty ground—dead. David, the brave shepherd boy became the next king of Israel. ❁

EDGAR A. GUEST

It Couldn't Be Done

Somebody said that it couldn't be done,

But he with a chuckle replied

That "maybe it couldn't," but he would be one

Who wouldn't say so till he'd tried.

So he buckled right in with the trace of a grin

On his face. If he worried he hid it.

He started to sing as he tackled the thing

That couldn't be done, and he did it.

Somebody scoffed: "Oh, you'll never do that;
At least no one ever has done it";
But he took off his coat and he took off his hat,
And the first thing we knew he'd begun it.
With a lift of his chin and a bit of a grin,
Without any doubting or quiddit,
He started to sing as he tackled the thing
That couldn't be done, and he did it.

There are thousands to tell you it cannot be done,

There are thousands to prophesy failure;

There are thousands to point out to you, one by one,

The dangers that wait to assail you.

But just buckle in with a bit of a grin,

Just take off your coat and go to it;

Just start to sing as you tackle the thing

That "cannot be done," and you'll do it.

THE BETTER PART OF VALOR IS DISCRETION.

SHAKESPEARE

If you want courage in any disaster,
Carefully, constantly follow the Master.
There's no discouragement that can make
you relent
Your promise, your intent, to be a pilgrim!

When people tell you you're fighting a lost war,
They just confuse themselves; your strength
will grow more.

You are God's chosen knight; though you with
giants fight,
You will make good your right to be a pilgrim.

Since God himself defends us with His Spirit
He guarantees the new life we'll inherit.
Lingering doubts, fly away! No matter what
you say,
I'll labor night and day to be a pilgrim. ❁

JOHN BUNYAN
"To Be a Pilgrim," paraphrased

Make up your mind not to worry beforehand how you will defend yourselves. For I will give you words and wisdom that none of your adversaries will be able to resist or contradict.... Not a hair of your head will perish. By standing firm you will save yourselves.

LUKE 21:14-18 NIV

Fear can keep a man out of danger, but courage can support him in it.

THOMAS FULLER

Courage is a quality so necessary for maintaining virtue that it is always respected.

SAMUEL JOHNSON

Act with courage, and may the Lord be with those who do well.

2 CHRONICLES 19:11 NIV

Have courage for the great sorrows of life and patience for the small ones. And when you have laboriously accomplished your daily task, go to sleep in peace. God is awake.

VICTOR HUGO

KEEP ALERT, STAND FIRM IN YOUR FAITH, BE COURAGEOUS, BE STRONG.

1 CORINTHIANS 16:13 NRSV

MARTIN LUTHER

a mighty fortress

A mighty fortress is our God,
A bulwark never failing;
Our helper He, amid the flood
Of mortal ills prevailing;
For still our ancient foe
Doth seek to work us woe;
His craft and power are great,
And, armed with cruel hate,
On earth is not his equal.

And though this world, with devils filled,
    Should threaten to undo us,
We will not fear, for God hath willed
    His truth to triumph through us:
The prince of darkness grim,
    We tremble not for him;
His rage we can endure,
    For lo, his doom is sure;
One little word shall fell him. ❁

A coward dies a thousand deaths;
the valiant dies but once.

SHAKESPEARE
Julius Caesar

He has not learned the lesson of life
who does not every day surmount
a fear.

RALPH WALDO EMERSON

Courage is almost a contradiction in terms. It means a strong desire to live taking the form of a readiness to die.

G. K. Chesterton

The one who endures to the end will be saved.

MATTHEW 24:13 NRSV

Where courage is not, no other virtue can survive except by accident.

SAMUEL JOHNSON

One man with courage makes a majority.

ANDREW JACKSON

Eight-year-old Glenn Cunningham raced into a burning schoolhouse to rescue his big brother. When he regained consciousness five hours later, his brother was dead and Glenn's horribly burned legs lay limp and without feeling. Specialists urged his parents to have Glenn's legs amputated immediately—he would never walk again—but Glenn pleaded against them. Even though the toes of his left foot were gone and the bone supporting the ball of his left foot practically destroyed, Glenn was determined to walk again.

That was the summer of 1919. One week later Glenn announced he was ready to stand up. His father lifted him out of bed, stood him upright and let go. Glenn crumpled to the floor. Every day Glenn's parents carefully rubbed his dead limbs. Every day for weeks, they repeated the lifting-falling exercise. Then one day, for a few seconds, Glenn Cunningham stood on his own.

A few days later Glenn took a few small, shaky steps. His parents kept on rubbing his legs. He ate carefully and began to push himself hard, running everywhere he went—to the fields, to the store, to school.

In 1930, with no toes on his left foot and almost missing a major bone, Glenn Cunningham set a high school record for the mile run, 4:24.7. He enrolled in Kansas University and two years later qualified for the Olympics with a United States record-setting mile of 4:11.1. Despite tonsillitis at the Los Angeles Olympics in 1932, he still finished fourth. He defeated milers around the world, repeatedly breaking his own records. In his early thirties he retired, holding the world mile record of 4:04.4. ❁

The only thing we have to fear is fear itself.

FRANKLIN DELANO ROOSEVELT
His first inaugural address, during the Great Depression

Keep conscience clear,
Then never fear.

BENJAMIN FRANKLIN

DO NOT PRAY
FOR EASY LIVES.
PRAY TO BE STRONGER.
DO NOT PRAY FOR TASKS
EQUAL TO YOUR POWERS.
PRAY FOR POWERS EQUAL
TO YOUR TASKS.

PHILLIPS BROOKS

I'm not afraid of the storm, for I'm learning how to sail my ship.

LOUISA MAY ALCOTT
Little Women

"Would you"—so the helmsman
answered,
"Learn the secret of the sea?
Only those who brave its dangers
Comprehend its mystery!"

HENRY WADSWORTH LONGFELLOW
The Secret of the Sea

If we take the generally accepted definition of bravery as a quality which knows not fear, I have never seen a brave man. All men are frightened. The more intelligent they are, the more they are frightened. The courageous man is the man who forces himself, in spite of his fear, to carry on. ❁

GEN. GEORGE S. PATTON, JR.
U.S. WORLD WAR II HERO

The courage to imagine the otherwise is our greatest resource, adding color and suspense to all our life.

DANIEL J. BOORSTIN

I think people are going to buy quite a passel of these gasoline buggies and they need gasoline to make 'em go. It may be the thing has a future.

FRANK PHILLIPS
FOUNDER OF PHILLIPS OIL COMPANY

Let liars fear, let cowards shrink,
Let traitors turn away,
Whatever we have dared to think
That dare we also say.

JAMES RUSSELL LOWELL

Tell a man he is brave, and you help him to become so.

THOMAS CARLYLE

Courage is when you do what you have to do though people don't think you can. Courage is when you think you can't do something, but you do it. Courage is when you are down and out and all the odds are against you, and you come out on top; it's when you stare your worst fear or toughest obstacle in the face and beat it. Courage is when you take on the impossible or fight an unwinnable fight. That's what courage is. ❁

ALAN McCORD
teenager paralyzed in an automobile accident

Courage is what it takes to stand up and speak; courage is also what it takes to sit down and listen.

WINSTON CHURCHILL

Behold the turtle. He makes progress only when he sticks his neck out.

JAMES BRYANT CONANT

COURAGE...IS WHEN YOU KNOW YOU'RE LICKED BEFORE YOU BEGIN BUT YOU BEGIN ANYWAY AND YOU SEE IT THROUGH NO MATTER WHAT.

HARPER LEE

Two roads diverged in a yellow wood,
And sorry I could not travel both
And be one traveler, long I stood
And looked down one as far as I could
To where it bent in the undergrowth;

Then took the other, as just as fair,
And having perhaps the better claim,
Because it was grassy and wanted wear;
Though as for that, the passing there
Had worn them really about the same,

And both that morning equally lay

In leaves no step had trodden black.

Oh, I kept the first for another day!

Yet knowing how way leads on to way,

I doubted if I should ever come back.

I shall be telling this with a sigh

Somewhere ages and ages hence:

Two roads diverged in a wood, and I—

I took the one less traveled by,

And that has made all the difference. ❁

ROBERT FROST, *The Road Less Traveled*

AESOP

The Brave Mice

An old cat was in the habit of catching all the mice in the barn.

One day the mice met to talk about the great harm that she was doing them. Each one told of some plan by which to keep out of her way.

"Do as I say," said an old gray mouse that was thought to be very wise. "Do as I say. Hang a bell to the cat's neck. Then, when we hear it ring, we shall know that she is coming, and can scamper out of her way."

"Good! Good!" said all the other mice, and one ran to get the bell.

"Now which of you will hang this bell on the cat's neck?" said the old gray mouse.

"Not I! Not I!" said all the mice together. And they scampered away to their holes. ❁

Jesus immediately said to them:

"Take courage! It is I. Don't be afraid."

MATTHEW 14:27 NIV

A man full of courage is also full of faith.

CICERO

COURAGE IS GRACE UNDER PRESSURE.

ERNEST HEMINGWAY

Be steadfast, immovable, always excelling.

1 CORINTHIANS 15:58 NRSV

Courage, the footstool of the Virtues, upon which they stand.

ROBERT LOUIS STEVENSON

Recall your courage, and lay aside sad fear.

VIRGIL

In valor there is hope.

TACITUS

The brave man is not he who feels
no fear,
For that were stupid and irrational;
but he whose noble soul its
fears subdues,
And bravely dares the danger nature
shrinks from.

JOANNA BAILLIE

If...

If you can keep your head when all about you
  Are losing theirs and blaming it on you;
If you can trust yourself when all men doubt you,
  But make allowance for their doubting too;
If you can wait and not be tired by waiting,
  Or, being lied about, don't deal in lies,
Or, being hated, don't give way to hating,
  And yet don't look too good, nor talk too wise;

If . . .

If you can dream—and not make dreams your master;
  If you can think—and not make thoughts your aim;
If you can meet with triumph and disaster
  And treat those two impostors just the same;
If you can bear to hear the truth you've spoken
  Twisted by knaves to make a trap of fools,
Or watch the things you gave your life to broken,
  And stoop and build 'em up with worn-out tools;

If you can make one heap of all your winnings
And risk it on one turn of pitch-and-toss,
And lose, and start again at your beginnings
And never breathe a word about your loss;
If you can force your heart and nerve and sinew
To serve your turn long after they are gone,
And so hold on when there is nothing in you
Except the Will which says to them: "Hold on."

If you can talk with crowds and keep your virtue,
Or walk with kings—nor lose the common touch;
If neither foes nor loving friends can hurt you;
If all men count with you, but none too much;
If you can fill the unforgiving minute
With sixty seconds' worth of distance run—
Yours is the Earth and everything that's in it,
And—which is more—you'll be a Man, my son!

RUDYARD KIPLING, *If*

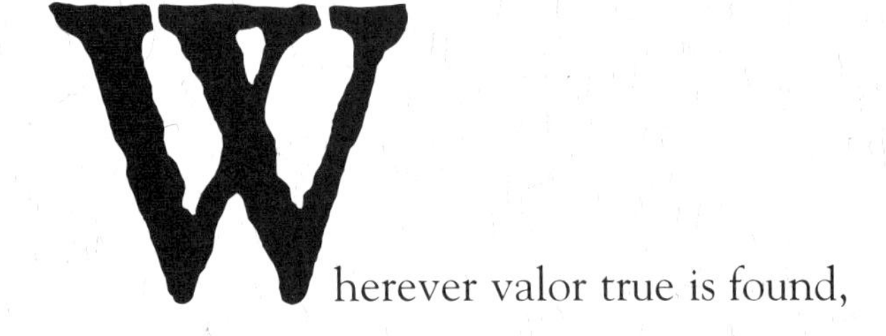

herever valor true is found,

True modesty will there abound.

W. S. GILBERT

Valor grows by daring, fear by holding back.

PUBLILIUS SYRUS

MOST ACTS OF ASSENT REQUIRE FAR MORE COURAGE THAN MOST ACTS OF PROTEST, SINCE COURAGE IS CLEARLY A READINESS TO RISK SELF-HUMILIATION.

NIGEL DENNIS

The mountains that inclose the vale
  With walls of granite, steep and high,
Invite the fearless foot to scale
  Their stairway toward the sky.

The restless, deep, dividing sea
  That flows and foams from shore to shore,
Calls to its sunburned chivalry,
  "Push out, set sail, explore!"

The bars of life at which we fret,

That seem to prison and control,

Are but the doors of daring, set

Ajar before the soul.

Say not, "Too poor," but freely give;

Sigh not, "Too weak," but boldly try;

You never can begin to live

Until you dare to die. ❁

HENRY VAN DYKE

Doors of Daring

I love the man that can smile in trouble, that can gather strength from distress, and grow brave by reflection...he whose heart is firm, and whose conscience approves his conduct, will pursue his principles unto death.

THOMAS PAINE

Screw your courage to the sticking-place,
And we'll not fail.

SHAKESPEARE

AS A FAVOR to his chief minister, Haman, King Xerxes of Persia ordered that all Jews be killed. Neither King Xerxes nor his chief minister, Haman, knew that Queen Esther was a Jew. Esther's uncle begged her to ask the king for mercy, but Esther was afraid. Going to the king without permission was illegal, even for her. Esther would be put to death, unless the king held out his gold scepter. But the king had not asked to see her for a whole month!

Esther's uncle pleaded, "Maybe this is the reason you are queen, for such a time as this."

"Pray for me. I will go to King Xerxes even

though it's against the law. And if I die, I die," Esther slowly answered.

Esther dressed in her royal robes and stepped, trembling, into the king's hall. When King Xerxes saw her, he extended his scepter. So Esther approached the king and touched the tip of his scepter.

"What is your request, Queen Esther?" asked the king.

"If it pleases the king," Esther carefully chose her words, "let the king and his servant, Haman, come to a banquet I will prepare."

The next day, the king and Haman went to dine

with Esther, and as they were reclining after their meal the king asked Esther to give him her request.

"If I have found favor with you," answered Esther, "grant me my life and spare my people—this is my request."

The king was terribly disturbed as Haman's deceptive plot to kill the Jews came unraveled. That same day, because of Esther's courage, the king canceled her death sentence and spared her people, and instead hanged his evil chief minister, Haman. ❁

retold from the book of Esther

Courage is the price that life exacts for
granting peace.
The soul that knows it not, knows no release
From little things;
Knows not the livid loneliness of fear,
Nor mountain heights where bitter joy can hear
The sound of wings.

AMELIA EARHART PUTNAM

COURAGE CONSISTS NOT IN HAZARDING WITHOUT FEAR, BUT BEING RESOLUTELY MINDED IN A JUST CAUSE.

PLUTARCH

Those who won our independence believed that the final end of the State was to make men free to develop their faculties.... They valued liberty both as an end and as a means. They believed liberty to be the secret of happiness and courage to be the secret of liberty.

LOUIS DEMBITZ BRANDEIS

Freedom is a system based on courage.

CHARLES PÉGUY

As courage and intelligence are the two qualifications best worth a good man's cultivation, so it is the first part of intelligence to recognize our precarious estate in life, and the first part of courage to be not at all abashed before the fact. ❖

ROBERT LOUIS STEVENSON

Courage is...

Courage is the virtue which champions the cause of right.

CICERO

Courage and resolution are the spirit and soul of virtue.

THOMAS FULLER

Courage is the knowledge of what ought to be endured.

PHILO

Integrity in all things precedes all else. The open demonstration of integrity is essential.

MAX DEPREE

That's courage—to take hard knocks like a man when occasion calls.

PLAUTUS

Real valor consists not in being insensible to danger, but in being prompt to confront and disarm it.

SIR WALTER SCOTT

I eagerly expect and hope that I will in no way be ashamed, but will have sufficient courage so that now as always Christ will be exalted in my body, whether by life or by death.

PHILIPPIANS 1:20 NIV

None but the brave deserves the fair.

JOHN DRYDEN

TRUE COURAGE IS TO DO WITHOUT WITNESSES EVERYTHING THAT ONE IS CAPABLE OF DOING BEFORE ALL THE WORLD.

LA ROCHEFOUCAULD

It is a brave act to despise death; but where life is more terrible than death, it is then the truest valor to dare to live.

SIR THOMAS BROWNE

Life only demands from you the strength you possess. Only one feat is possible—not to have run away.

DAG HAMMARSKJÖLD

With malice toward none, with charity for all, with firmness in the right as God gives us to see the right, let us finish the work we are in, to bind up the nation's wounds, to care for him who shall have borne the battle, and for his widow and orphans, to do all which may achieve and cherish a just and lasting peace among ourselves and with all nations. ❁

ABRAHAM LINCOLN
from his second inaugural address

LONG, LONG AGO, there was an emperor who spent his fortune on beautiful clothes. One fine day two strangers offered to weave the king the most beautiful clothing ever made. These clothes would be so beautiful that they would be invisible to any people who were stupid or did not deserve their jobs.

The impostors pretended to weave invisible cloth and everyone admired its beauty for fear of looking foolish. The emperor's servants pretended to dress him in the imaginary clothes, and out he went to parade through the city in his new clothes. All along the procession, the emperor's subjects cheered and clapped and shouted how wonderful the new clothes looked.

Then a little child said, "The emperor isn't wearing any clothes." And the whole crowd began to say the same thing. ❁

HANS CHRISTIAN ANDERSEN
The Emperor's New Clothes

Sometimes even to live is an act of courage.

SENECA

What hangs in the balance is nowise in doubt;
We know the event and we brave what we know.

ANNA AKHMATOVA

Lad, you took the world's soul,
Thrilled it by your daring,
Lifted the uncaring
And made them joyous men.

ANGELA MORGAN

You have to accept whatever comes, and the only important thing is that you meet it with courage and with the best that you have to give.

ELEANOR ROOSEVELT

Any coward can fight a battle when he's sure of winning; but give me the man who has pluck to fight when he's sure of losing. That's my way, sir; and there are many victories worse than a defeat.

GEORGE ELIOT

TO DIE FOR THE REVOLUTION IS A ONE-SHOT DEAL; TO LIVE FOR THE REVOLUTION MEANS TAKING ON THE MORE DIFFICULT COMMITMENT OF CHANGING OUR DAY-TO-DAY LIFE PATTERNS.

FRANCES M. BEAL

EDGAR GUEST

The Things that Haven't Been Done Before

The things that haven't been done before,
Those are the things to try;
Columbus dreamed of an unknown shore
At the rim of the far-flung sky,
And his heart was bold and his faith was strong
As he ventured in dangers new,
And he paid no heed to the jeering throng
Or the fears of the doubting crew.

The many will follow the beaten track
With guideposts on the way.
They live and have lived for ages back
With a chart for every day.
Someone has told them it's safe to go
On the road he has traveled o'er,
And all they ever strive to know
Are the things that were known before.

A few strike out, without map or chart,
Where never a man has been,
From the beaten paths they draw apart
To see what no man has seen.
There are deeds they hunger alone to do;
Though battered and bruised and sore,
They blaze the path for the many, who
Do nothing not done before.

The things that haven't been done before
Are the tasks worthwhile today;
Are you one of the flock that follows, or
Are you one that shall lead the way?
Are you one of the timid souls that quail
At the jeers of a doubting crew,
Or dare you, whether you win or fail,
Strike out for a goal that's new? ❁

The visibility of courage is very much heightened during the times of crisis and turmoil. But there are other less visible forms of courage—courage to do your best each day when there are no mountain top experiences to keep you going; courage to say no when "everyone is doing it"; courage to permit compromise; courage to stand your ground on things that should not be compromised.

LES SONNABEND

Courage is knowing what to fear.

Plato

Courage is not simply one of the virtues, but the form of every virtue at the testing point, which means, at the point of highest reality. A chastity or honesty or mercy which yields to danger will be chaste or honest or merciful only on conditions. Pilate was merciful 'til it became risky. ❁

C. S. LEWIS

The Screwtape Letters

My sword I give to him that shall succeed me in my pilgrimage, and my courage and skill to him that can get it. My marks and scars I carry with me, to be a witness for me, that I have fought His battles who now will be my rewarder.

JOHN BUNYAN